AF413461
THIS JOURNAL BELONGS TO

"I've got the key to my castle in the air,

but whether I can unlock the door remains

to be seen."

"Love is a great beautifier."

"Watch and pray, dear, never get tired of trying, and never think it is impossible to conquer your fault."

"I like good strong words that mean something."

"Be worthy, love, and love will come."

"I'll try and be what he loves to call me, 'a little woman,'
and not be rough and wild; but do my duty here instead
of wanting to be somewhere else."

"Don't try and make me grow up
before my time."

"Take some books and read; that's an immense help;
and books are always good company if you
have the right sort."

"Conceit spoils the finest genius."

"Life and love are very precious when both are in
full bloom."

"When you feel discontented, think over your blessings,
and be grateful."

"Now and then, in this workaday world, things do happen in
the delightful storybook fashion, and what a comfort it is."

"I don't like to doze by the fire. I like adventures,
and I'm going to find some."

"I think you will prosper, for the sincere
wish to be good is half the battle."

UN
SQ
gift
UNION
SQUARE
& CO.
NEW YORK